Hi! I'm Cliff Richard, and I'm taking time out in the middle of a concert tour to share something with you which, without exaggerating, must be the most crucial issue that a person can ever face. Certainly in my life it's top priority, with rock 'n' roll and tennis in another league! What I'm talking about is becoming a Christian – and, in a sense, that's a matter of life or death.

First of all, I'll lay my cards on the table – I'm no spiritual expert, so don't expect heavy theology! What I have got is a Christian conversion experience that happened when I was twenty-four, and that changed my outlook and my life. Since then I've notched up . . . well, a year or two's experience of living as a Christian in a busy and pressurised modern world. Very simply, I believe that conversion – or rebirth, as the Bible calls it – is possible and necessary for everyone if they want to live life to the full, and I want to explain it as best I can, because it's too good and too important to keep to myself.

Be prepared for a few religious words and phrases. I can't avoid them. I know the thought of 'conversion' might make you a little uneasy for starters, but all that means is 'a change'. I'm thinking of converting my central heating at home, for instance, from an oil to a gas system. Spiritual conversion is about a change from a self-centred life system to one that is Jesus-centred. I remember hearing a preacher once say that becoming a Christian isn't a new start in life, but a new life to start. Clever, those preachers!

There are many, of course, who doubt whether Christian conversions are for real. They're either the product of a quirky imagination, they say, or some gigantic effort of will power. Let me tell you that, if my conversion was imagination, then so is this chair I'm sitting on! My life isn't about make-believe. As I·say, it's busy, often bombarded from all directions, and very active! I don't have time for chasing fantasies or for lifestyles that don't work.

A Real Experience

What happened to me back in 1964 wasn't fiction, but an experience that altered me as a person, complete with priorities, attitudes and choices. Of course my own psychological make-up was involved in the change as well, but that doesn't diminish or explain away what happened. Quite the reverse! 'Imagination' is too feeble and totally inadequate an explanation, while the 'will power' argument is just too ludicrous. My New Year's resolutions last a week, if I'm ultra-careful. Mere resolves to live like a Christian by my own efforts and determination result in failure and frustration. 'I've tried it,' people say, 'and it didn't work.' Of course it didn't. Christianity isn't something we try to do – it's a Person we have to meet. There's a verse in the Bible that says, 'He who has the Son has life; he who has not the Son of God has not life' (1 John 5:12). Black and white, that. No sitting on the fence, no hint of 'I'll make it if I'm good'. You either have this new life or you haven't. You either have Jesus or yc haven't!

The best way I can explain how to become a Christian is to describe what I went through because, although we're all different and all approach God with different needs and attitudes, God's plan is the same for all of us.

I was never an atheist. Even as a kid I believed there was someone 'up there' who must have set the whole universe going. It was all too fantastic to believe that everything was just one huge purposeless accident. But that's as far as it went. God had nothing to do with me and, although I'd resort to the occasional SOS type or crisis prayer, He was never real and religion was much the same as walking around ladders instead of under them!

Much More To Life

It was a few years into my show-business career when I first sensed a sort of incompleteness. I don't know how else to put it. It was as though there was something more to life, despite the fact that I had so much going for me. Certainly as much fame, fortune and popularity as any one person could handle. The girls screamed, hits came regularly, accountants were employed to cope with the income, but, despite all that, it didn't add up to satisfaction. When I went home and took off the public 'mask', which I guess we all wear some of the time, I still had to live with the real me. And, although I don't suppose I was any worse – or any better, come to that – than the next bloke, I knew that success, fans and money were no compensation for being restless deep within myself.

Now I certainly wouldn't dare suggest that you take my experience as any sort of blueprint unless it could be backed up and checked out from the Bible, and, in this instance, Isaiah in the Old Testament reflects exactly what I was going through. Those who reject God he says, 'are like the restless sea, which is never still . . . there is no peace . . . for them' (Isa. 57:20–1). Does that ring any bells?

The Heart Of The Problem

It was a few years later before I really understood the reason for this restlessness. You'll know the word – although you won't like it any more than I did. Sin. That's the problem. More serious than naughtiness, and more profound than disobedience or imperfection, it's a condition we inherit, it spoils our life and our relationships and, most disastrous of all, it separates us from God. There's no purpose in comparing our sin with someone else's and reckoning we're 'not so bad', because in God's sight there are no degrees. All your good deeds are like 'filthy rags', writes Isaiah (64:6). And, straight from the shoulder, the Apostle Paul tells us that 'all have sinned and fall short of the glory of God' (Rom. 3:23). No exceptions, no Divine favourites – all of us are tarred with the same brush and, what's more, all of us know it. I have yet to meet a person who is arrogant enough to think he's perfect and, if you're truthfully in any doubt, then measure yourself against God's rulebook. When we take an honest look at ourselves we're not too impressed by what we see. It's just more socially acceptable to keep the window well dressed!

That's the problem then. God, who is perfect justice, perfect goodness, and perfect everything else, and me, who is full of selfishness and disobedience. Like light and darkness, the two can't mix. Quite separate and totally irreconcilable, except for one amazing, marvellous fact – God loves me and wants me in His family.

True Love
Again, it took a long while before the truth dawned, and literally for years I kept up a barrage of questions and argument. Looking back, I'm grateful that there were those around me who could not only answer, but who were able to put God's love into practice. Actions always speak louder than words, and somehow I saw in their lives what was patiently and repeatedly explained to me. 'For God so loved the world that He gave His one and only Son, that whoever believes in Him shall not perish but have eternal life' (John 3:16).

This was God's way of loving us without excusing us. His law had been broken and it was impossible for God to turn a blind eye but, instead of imposing a penalty on us law-breakers, Jesus died, 'the just for the unjust, that He might bring us to God' (1 Pet. 3:18). That's why the cross is so central to the Christian faith. Many preachers have said it's as though all our sins – all that we have done and all that we haven't done that has displeased God – were nailed on the cross along with Jesus and wiped out from God's memory. Just ponder that for a moment – it's mind-blowing! 'He has removed our sins as far away

4

from us as the east is from the west,' wrote David (Ps. 103:12). The whole Calvary story is amazing, and the more you dig into its parallels with the Old Testament practices of sacrifices for sin, the more profound and meaningful the crucifixion of Jesus becomes.

Of course it was an event that changed history, but remember – it only changed history because it changed people. Individuals who realised that, because of the cross, they could be forgiven, whatever their past and whatever their failure. The same applies to you.

Although I have no idea who will be reading this, I am certain that Jesus' death is as relevant for you as for me – but have you made it work for yourself yet? It's like some magnificent meal – full of protein, vitamins and goodness, everything that's essential for health and energy. For both of us exactly the same potential – but effective only for the one who eats.

Need For Commitment

Anyway, back to my story, and all those questions that I fussed about for so long. I knew my life wasn't right and I wanted to change. I accepted that Jesus' death was somehow the key to it all and, what's more, I believed that Jesus wasn't a dusty character from history. Dead people might still have an influence but they don't change lives. And I had little intellectual problem in believing that Jesus was, in some strange miraculous way, still alive. For a start, the eye-witness evidence given to us in the Bible is overwhelming and, although the mind can't comprehend the mechanics of the resurrection, it's surely not illogical to accept that the Creator God should have power even over death.

And do you see what a massive difference it makes to actually being a Christian if we can relate to a living person rather than cling to a philosophical system? Being a Christian isn't obeying a code of ethics, although discipline and obedience are certainly involved. It isn't dependent upon our resources of will power, and it's certainly nothing to do with notching up so many church attendances.

Christianity is commitment to Jesus; it's about knowing Him as a living, personal and intimate friend, and about serving Him as our Lord and God.

I started that commitment, and I discovered later a new lifestyle, when I lay on my bed one night in the mid-sixties and prayed very simply that Jesus would come into the life of Cliff Richard and save it and rule over it. I'd gone as far as I could with questions and answers and theories and arguments. Now the things I believed with my head had to extend to my heart and my life. Jesus' words in the last book of the Bible – Revelation 3:20 – focussed it for me. 'Behold, I stand at the door and knock,' says Jesus, 'if anyone hears my voice and opens the door, I will come in to him.'

All I can do in this little booklet is commend Jesus to you. If you're conscious of Him knocking, so to speak, then please respond. There's a new dimension of life ahead for you if you do, although not all straightforward and problem-free. Far from it! Christian commitment always has been and still is costly, and I'm sure there will be personal pressures for you if you take that step – but the other side of the coin is that now there are two of you – a marvellous, potential-loaded partnership of you and Jesus. And, while He won't steer you around life's problems, He'll certainly guide and hold you through them.

How do you open the door? Simply invite Him to take over and trust that, by His Spirit, He'll do it. Revelation 3:20 is a promise, and it's unambiguous. 'If *anyone* hears my voice and opens the door, I *will* come in.' After my prayer there were no dramas, no flashing lights or booming voices – just a quiet sense of peace and a hint of excitement. Twenty years later, the peace is deeper and the excitement greater.

When It's Time For Commitment

I'm not going to suggest the exact words of a prayer, because that needs to be your expression – and, remember, God isn't bothered about well-structured sentences! But you should tell God you need Him and are prepared to change your life as He directs and enables you. Then accept all He is offering you as an unconditional free gift – forgiveness, a new dimension of life, and the power to live it. And don't forget to thank Him for loving you!

If and when you pray like that, try to find another Christian to tell. It will help you, delight them, and enable others to pray for you and encourage you.

Below are some Bible verses which will help sharpen the focus of what I have tried to explain, but remember – becoming a Christian is a beginning, not an end. Just as a new baby needs to learn and develop and grow, so do you. There are three essentials.

1. Get to know your new Friend by talking with Him regularly. Praying isn't just for church. Some of my best chat sessions are when I'm out walking the dogs!

2. Get stuck into reading and understanding the Bible. Hard going it may be in places, but it will be an eye-opener, as well as necessary nourishment. I suggest you start by reading a book in the New Testament, say Luke or John.

3. Recognise that you have a new family and start to enjoy them. Like any family, some are a bit way out, but Christians have a deep and special bond, and meeting together to worship your Father is natural and enriching. In other words, find a good church where you feel at home, and join it. It needs you as much as you need it!

Check out these references in your Bible: if you don't have one most bookshops stock a modern translation.

About you and sin: Romans 3:23, Isaiah 59:2, Isaiah 53:6, 1 John 1:5,6.
About you and forgiveness: Isaiah 1:18, Acts 10:43, Matthew 26:28.
About you and the crucifixion: 2 Corinthians 5:21, Isaiah 53:5,6, 1 Peter 2:24, 1 Peter 3:18, John 3:16.
About you and the resurrection: Matthew 28:6, 1 Corinthians 15:17–20, Philippians 3:10.
About you and your response: Revelation 3:20, Acts 16:31, Acts 2:38,39, Psalms 34:8, Matthew 11:28–30.
About you and a new life: 1 John 5:12, John 1:12, John 16, Philippians 4:13, 1 Corinthians 10:13, 2 Corinthians 12:9.

British Library Cataloguing in Publication Data

Richard, Cliff
   Mine to share.–(Hodder Christian paperback)
   1. Christian life
   I. Title
   248.4   BV4501.2

   ISBN 0 340 36097 6